NO WAY! Spectacular Sports Stories

D1310070

Monika Davies

Consultants

Timothy Rasinski, Ph.D.
Kent State University

Lori Oczkus, M.A.
Literacy Consultant

Publishing Credits

Rachelle Cracchiolo, M.S.Ed., *Publisher*

Conni Medina, M.A.Ed., *Managing Editor*

Dona Herweck Rice, *Series Developer*

Emily R. Smith, M.A.Ed., *Content Director*

Stephanie Bernard/Susan Daddis, M.A.Ed., *Editors*

Robin Erickson, *Senior Graphic Designer*

The TIME logo is a registered trademark of TIME Inc. Used under license.

Image Credits: Cover and p.1 Philip Oldham/Cal Sport Media/Newscom; pp.6, 8, 12–13 John Biever/Sports Illustrated/Getty Images; p.9 Ronald C. Modra/Sports Imagery/Getty Images; pp.14–15 LOC [LC-DIG-ggbain-21542]; p.16 B Bennett/Getty Images; p.18 Aflo Co. Ltd./Alamy Stock Photo; p.19 Photo by: Melinda Sue Gordon/Production Co.s: Scott Rudin Productions/Michael De Luca Productions/Plan B Entertainment/ AF archive/Alamy Stock Photo; p.20 Springfield College, Babson Library, Archives and Special Collections; p.23 (back) Copyright 2013 NBAE (Photo by Ned Dishman/NBAE via Getty Images), (front) Copyright 2004 WNBAE (Photo by D. Clarke Evans/NBAE via Getty Images); p.25 Copyright 2003 NBAE (Photo by Andrew D. Bernstein/NBAE/Getty Images); p.26 David E. Klutho/Sports Illustrated/Getty Images; p.28 Dave Sandford/Getty Images; p.29 Creative Commons File:Stanley Cup, 2015.jpg by Alex Goykhman used under CC BY-SA 4.0; p.30 Dave Sandford/Getty Images; pp.32–33 Popperfoto/Getty Images; pp.34–35 Bob Thomas/Popperfoto/Getty Images; pp.36, 38 Michael Regan/Getty Images; p.39 GLYN KIRK/AFP/Getty Images; p.41 Razzle-dazzle/Wikimedia Commons/Public Domain; all other images from iStock and/or Shutterstock.

All teams, companies, and/or products mentioned in this book are registered trademarks of their respective owners or developers and are used in this book strictly for editorial purposes. No commercial claim to their use is made by the author or the publisher.

Note: The answers to the mathematics problems posed throughout this book are provided on page 48.

Teacher Created Materials
5301 Oceanus Drive
Huntington Beach, CA 92649-1030
http://www.tcmpub.com
ISBN 978-1-4938-3609-3
© 2017 Teacher Created Materials, Inc.

Table of Contents

The Weird, Wild, and Wonderful

Imagine sitting in a seat in a packed stadium. You're surrounded by thousands of excited, screaming fans. You start conversations with people around you, asking, "Who are you cheering for?" The game begins. Just as you think your team is about to win, the opponents swoop in and take the lead. You become completely captivated, and you get a rush of **adrenaline** when the game gets too close to call.

The most entertaining part of watching a sport, be it tennis, hockey, or football, is how **unpredictable** a game can be. We can examine statistics and make guesses about what will happen, but many of the finest moments in sports come as surprises to spectators.

In honor of the sporting world's unpredictability, we will delve into some of the most exciting sports moments in history. There will be number crunching and lots of head scratching. You might even think we are making these numbers up. (Please feel free to double-check—we promise we are telling the truth!)

It's a Numbers Game!

Do you love sports and math? If so, you should learn about sports **statisticians**. Sports are all about numbers, and there are people who keep statistics for everything. For example, in the 2015–16 regular season, professional basketball player Stephen Curry made 402 out of 886 three-point baskets. He shattered his own record of 286 three-pointers from the previous season. What was his shooting percentage from beyond the three-point line?

The Biggest Comeback in NFL History

You are halfway through one of the most important football games of the season. A peek at the scoreboard reveals that your team is down 32 points. The chance of your team winning seems impossibly slim.

While it can be tempting to give up when your team is trailing so far behind, take heart and look back to the most spectacular comeback in National Football League (NFL) history.

Warren Moon

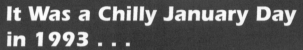

Football Factory

Over 700,000 footballs are made yearly at the Wilson Football Factory in Ada, Ohio, exclusively for the NFL. If 2,800 footballs are made each business day, how many days per year is the factory open?

It Was a Chilly January Day in 1993 . . .

The January 3, 1993, matchup between the Buffalo Bills and the Houston Oilers was to be remembered as the wildest of all **wild card** games. Set in Buffalo, New York, the game **pitted** the two teams against each other, and both were eager to keep their Super Bowl dreams alive.

The first half of the game was a showcase for the skills of Warren Moon, the Oilers' quarterback. Moon completed 19 out of 22 passes, and his commanding performance yielded four touchdowns. The Bills were down 28–3 by halftime. The Oilers controlled over 21 minutes of **possession** in the first 30 minutes of the game and owned both the field and the scoreboard.

Coming to You Live!

The first time a football game scored its way onto a television screen was in 1939. The viewing audience was fewer than 5,000 for that illustrious first game. Now compare—the average televised Super Bowl game today has over 100 million viewers!

When the players returned for the second half, the Bills still seemed down on their luck. Within the first two minutes of the third quarter, the Oilers **intercepted** a Bills' play and quickly scored another touchdown. The Bills were now down a seemingly hopeless 35–3. Buffalo fans had already begun to leave the stadium, predicting there was no way the Bills could come back from such a huge **deficit**. They were mistaken.

A Comeback Like No Other

With little more than 13 minutes to go in the third quarter, the **momentum** began to shift slowly. The Bills scored their first touchdown of the game, driving 50 yards in 10 plays.

All eyes were on the next play when the Bills' kicker Steve Christie recovered his onside kick. The end result was a 38-yard touchdown pass. Frank Reich, the Bills' quarterback, had been shaky from the game's beginning but was starting to build plays with confidence.

On the football field, wild weather can force teams to rethink strategy, such as during the **infamous** December 31, 1988, "Fog Bowl." The fog during this crazy game, played in Chicago, was so thick that players could barely see where they were going, let alone a ball hurtling toward them.

◉ What would you do in this scenario as a player? How about as a coach or an official?

◉ What would be the worst weather conditions to play football in?

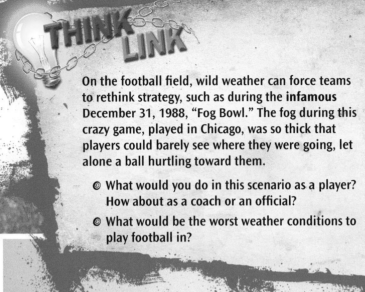

What Is an Onside Kick?

An onside kick is when a team deliberately completes a short kickoff, and the ball must travel a minimum of 10 yards. The kicking team then tries to recover the ball so that it has possession again. It is a very risky play but a potential game changer for a team trying to catch up.

The Buffalo Bills were tackling the game with renewed energy and hope, and they promptly scored two more touchdowns.

It took the Bills a grand total of six minutes and 52 seconds to claw their way back from a 32-point deficit. They were now a mere four points down, had scored four touchdowns in less than seven minutes, and were staring down a decidedly nervous Oilers team. The score was 35–31 in favor of the Oilers.

On the Edges of Our Seats

There were less than five minutes to play in **regulation** when the Bills scored their fifth touchdown of the game and pulled ahead of the Oilers for the first time. They were now three points ahead, and the Bills' fans had been whipped into a feverish frenzy.

But the Oilers were not going to let the game slip away from them that easily.

Count It Out!

Active play
11 minutes

Replays
15 minutes

Shots of players standing around
67 minutes

Commercials
63 minutes

Shots of coaches/crowd/cheerleaders
35 minutes

STOP! THINK...

A typical televised football game lasts about 3 hours and 11 minutes. Official game play is 60 minutes in four 15-minute quarters. But actual active play time only totals about 11 minutes! Remember, the clock often runs in between plays. Look at how 191 minutes of airtime add up, and then answer the questions.

- What percentage of a football broadcast is active play time?

- How does active play time compare to commercial time or shots of players?

- How do you think commentators should handle "dead air" and keep the audience entertained?

The seconds were ticking down when the Oilers tied the game with a field goal. The game headed into overtime—something no one could have foreseen at halftime.

Overtime and Over-the-Moon Bills' Fans

Tension was high as the Oilers won the coin flip. However, any luck the Oilers had quickly evaporated. The Bills intercepted the ball in Oilers' territory, and suddenly, victory was within kicking distance for the Bills.

The Bills scored a 32-yard field goal three minutes and six seconds into overtime, and the NFL's most spectacular comeback ended with a final score of 41–38. It was a game for the history books.

The next time you see a lopsided score, remember the Bills. There really is no better reminder of the age-old advice, "Never give up!"

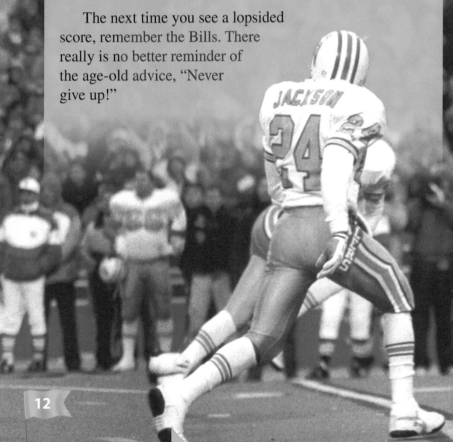

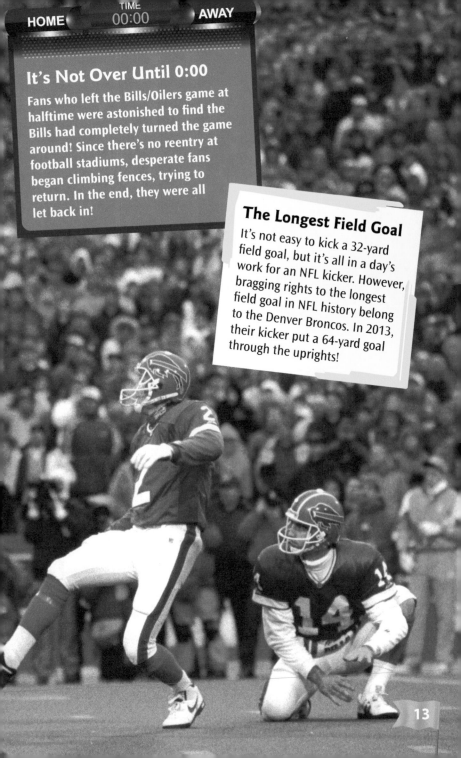

It's Not Over Until 0:00

Fans who left the Bills/Oilers game at halftime were astonished to find the Bills had completely turned the game around! Since there's no reentry at football stadiums, desperate fans began climbing fences, trying to return. In the end, they were all let back in!

The Longest Field Goal

It's not easy to kick a 32-yard field goal, but it's all in a day's work for an NFL kicker. However, bragging rights to the longest field goal in NFL history belong to the Denver Broncos. In 2013, their kicker put a 64-yard goal through the uprights!

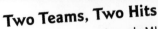

Two Teams, Two Hits

Joel Youngblood is the only MLB player to get hits for two different teams on the same day. On August 4, 1982, he started at Wrigley Field for the Mets, where he went one for two at the plate. He left in the third inning with the news that he'd been traded to the Montreal Expos. Youngblood showered, ate dinner, and flew to Philadelphia to play for his new team. He arrived in the third inning and had a hit in his only at bat!

Iron Man

On September 20, 1998, Cal Ripken made the decision to end his streak of 2,632 consecutive games played in Major League Baseball. He started all of those games in a Baltimore Orioles uniform. The previous record was 2,130 games held by "The Iron Horse," Lou Gehrig.

The Longest Undefeated Streaks in Baseball

Winning streaks are legendary. Stringing a row of wins together is difficult to accomplish in any sport, which makes winning streaks rare and unique.

In baseball, an undefeated streak is not the result of one person carrying a team to repeated victories. Instead, it means an entire team is knocking game after game out of the park.

1916 New York Giants

The longest undefeated streak in Major League Baseball (MLB) history belongs to the New York Giants. The 1916 team went an astonishing 26 games without a single loss. This streak is even more incredible considering it was the second one that season. Only a few months earlier, the Giants had a winning streak of 17 games in a row.

Some people are quick to point out that this is not the longest *winning* streak. The Giants had a single tie tucked in the middle of the 26 games. However, the most **wonky** part of this season is that the Giants finished fourth in the National League! Despite *two* major winning streaks, the 1916 Giants finished with a disappointing 86–66 record.

1935 Chicago Cubs

The record holder for the longest undefeated streak in MLB history is widely debated. Non-Giants fans will direct your attention to the 1935 Chicago Cubs as the true record holder.

The 1935 Cubs were a talented team, and their season record proved their potential. That year, they had a winning streak of 21 games. Unlike the 1916 Giants, not a single tie broke their winning momentum. They also won 100 games in the season—a **feat** that teams still strive for today. The team would go on to become National League Champions.

1935 Cubs pitchers: Larry French, Lon Warneke, Bill Lee, and Charlie Root

Sadly, their tremendous season closed on a sour note. The Cubs headed to the World Series with high expectations, but they were unable to continue their success. Their opponents, the Detroit Tigers, claimed the World Series title in Game 6.

Muddy Hands

Did you know there is no such thing as a **pristine** major league baseball? Every ball is coated with mud from a secret location along the Delaware River to give it better grip!

HOME | TIME 00:00 | AWAY

Calculating Batting Average

To calculate a player's batting average, take his number of base hits and divide that by the total number of official at bats. A player's average is counted to three decimal places. Babe Ruth's career batting average was 0.342, and his total number of at bats was 8,399. Using these figures, how many base hits did Ruth get in his career?

2002 Oakland Athletics

Perhaps the most inspiring winning streak is one from the early twenty-first century. The "small budget team that could," the 2002 Oakland Athletics (A's), had a season that still sparks conversation.

Baseball Stats

Determining statistics in sports has a lot to do with math. One of the most important statistics in baseball today is the OPS. This stands for *on-base (percentage) plus slugging (average)*. In other words, how often does the player get on base and hit for power? The best hitters in the MLB have an OPS of about 0.95.

Facing the departure of three key players, the A's had an uncertain future. The team did not have a deep budget to court big name players, so they **reinvented** their strategy to sign new ones. They began choosing players with high **on-base percentages** to round out their roster.

The Oakland A's went on to have an amazing season. The highlight was their 20-game winning streak, an American League record. Unfortunately, winning streaks do not guarantee championship titles. The A's ended their season losing in the opening round of the playoffs.

Moneyball

To learn more about the Oakland A's game-changing season, read Michael Lewis's book *Moneyball: The Art of Winning an Unfair Game*. If a film is more up your alley, *Moneyball* the movie was released in 2011.

The Highest-Scoring Basketball Game

There are very few basketball games that can lay claim to breaking multiple National Basketball Association (NBA) records in one fell swoop. However, if you backpedal into the '80s, you will stumble upon an NBA game with jaw-dropping statistics—the December 13, 1983, matchup between the Detroit Pistons and the Denver Nuggets.

Peachy Keen

Before the creation of **symmetrical** steel-and-aluminum hoops with nylon nets, players shot baskets into very different kinds of nets. The first basketball players actually scored in peach baskets!

Basketball Overtimes

A regulation NBA game contains four quarters that are each twelve minutes long. If the score is tied at the end of the game, the two teams then enter an overtime period, which is five minutes long. How long would a basketball game be if it included six overtimes?

A Standard Start

This record-breaking game started off without great fanfare but was a good matchup. The Pistons and Nuggets were both hot on offense, exchanging points back and forth. It appeared both teams could not miss a shot. At halftime, the teams were tied 74–74 and were still running rapidly up and down the court. By the end of regulation, the score had leaped to 145–145. It was a sizable score, but no one was rushing to alert the record books. The NBA record for the highest-scoring game at the time was still 47 points away.

Then the overtimes began.

Eye-Popping Overtimes

The first overtime started with the Nuggets pulling ahead. The win seemed to be within their grasp. But the Pistons responded with a nimble run, scoring their only three-pointer of the night to tie the game at 159–159.

Both teams wanted the game to end, but neither was willing to back down. Nuggets' player Kelly Tripucka scored 12 points in the second overtime, and the Pistons matched him point for point. The game was tied again, 171–171. The record for the highest-scoring NBA game had officially been broken— and the game was still on!

In the third overtime, with just over a minute left, the Pistons took the lead. The game ended after three hours of play with an astonishing score of 186–184, tipped in the Detroit Pistons' favor.

Startling Statistics

That 1983 game tallied up seven NBA records. These include the most points scored by two teams (370) and the most points scored by one team (186). Four different players scored over 40 points each! Most NBA teams score around 100 points per game, so breaking these records will be difficult for any team to achieve.

Spin-tastic!

Michael Kettman is known for setting the world record for most basketballs spun simultaneously. He was able to spin 28 basketballs, all at the same time, using a PVC pipe rig with pointed nails and his fingers. Pretty impressive!

Margo Dydek

STARS

12

Shannon Bobbitt

INOVA

WNBA Heights

Professional female basketball players play in the Women's National Basketball Association (WNBA). Margo Dydek holds the record for being the tallest WNBA player in history at 7 feet 2 inches (2.18 meters). Standing a full two feet (0.61 meters) shorter than Dydek is Shannon Bobbitt, 5'2", the shortest WNBA player in history.

Height vs. Shoe Size

Basketball players are not only known for their sky-high heights but also for owning some of the largest shoes on Earth. Let's look at some of the world's best players and how their heights compare to their shoe sizes.

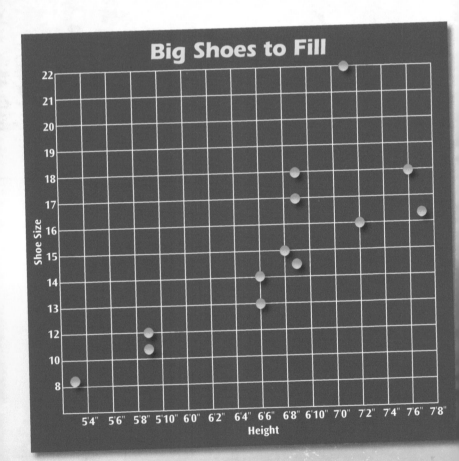

Name	Height	Shoe Size
Muggsy Bogues	5'3" (63")	8.5
Nate Robinson	5'9" (69")	10.5
Isaiah Thomas	5'9" (69")	12
Michael Jordan	6'6" (78")	13
Kobe Bryant	6'6" (78")	14
LeBron James	6'8" (80")	15
Carmelo Anthony	6'8" (80")	15
Larry Bird	6'9" (81")	17
Magic Johnson	6'9" (81")	14.5
Kevin Durant	6'9" (81")	18
Shaquille O'Neal	7'1" (85")	22
Kareem Abdul-Jabbar	7'2" (86")	16
Yao Ming	7'6" (90")	18
Manute Bol	7'7" (91")	16.5

Shaquille O'Neal's shoe

Answer these questions using the graph:

1. Based on the scatter plot, what is the correlation between a player's height and his shoe size?

2. Are there any outliers on the graph? Why would they be considered outliers?

3. Using the first five players in the table, determine the average ratio of height to shoe size. Round your answers to two decimal places. Hint: You must find the ratio for each individual player first.

The First Outdoor NHL Game

Ice hockey was born on the frosty outdoor rinks of Canada, but in the past, National Hockey League (NHL) games were always played indoors. An outdoor NHL game was a dream for both players and fans for many years; however, the idea seemed far fetched. That was the case until 2003, when the Canadian city of Edmonton hosted the Heritage Classic.

The 2003 Heritage Classic

The historic event was to feature two games. The first would be the headline of the event, a Legends Game. It matched up former members of the Edmonton Oilers and the Montreal Canadiens. The second game would have current players for both teams. The Legends Game would have some of hockey's greatest players facing off again, including Wayne Gretzky and Guy Lafleur. There was a mountain of excitement behind the event. Gretzky's name alone inspired much of the **anticipation**. However, before this dream could become a reality, a rink was needed.

Hockey Darlings

Some countries—Canada, Russia, and the United States, for instance—are known as hockey darlings. And they have the rinks to prove it! Take a peek at the surprising statistics for the five countries with the most indoor and outdoor rinks.

Country	Number of Indoor Rinks	Number of Outdoor Rinks
Canada	2,631	5,000
Russia	450	2,553
United States	1,900	500
Sweden	358	136
Finland	260	24

Source: www.iihf.com/iihf-home/countries

STOP! THINK...

Use the data from Hockey Darlings to answer the questions.

- Why do certain countries have more outdoor rinks than indoor rinks?

- What do these countries have in common besides their love of hockey?

Most major cities in North America have several indoor hockey arenas. But how do you find an outdoor rink that meets NHL arena standards and can accommodate over 50,000 fans? You build it.

It was decided to host the event on the football field in Edmonton's Commonwealth Stadium, which could hold about 60,000 fans. The transformation of the field to an ice rink started with the following materials:

- 35 trucks full of sand
- 1,000 plywood sheets
- 800 feet of pipe
- 205 tons of refrigerated **brine**
- 70 rink boards
- 120 Plexiglas® sections
- 100 workers

Workers prepare Commonwealth Stadium days ahead of the Heritage Classic.

The plywood was set down first, followed by the sand. The pipes were then laid on top and were pumped full of refrigerated brine to make sure the ice would freeze properly. It took 12 days for the 100 crew members to create the makeshift outdoor rink.

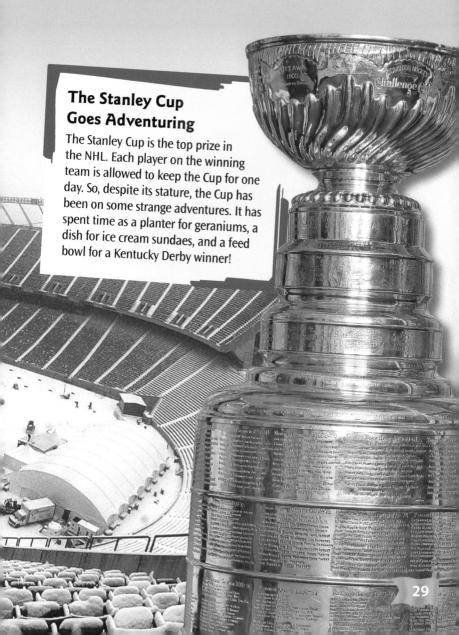

The Stanley Cup Goes Adventuring

The Stanley Cup is the top prize in the NHL. Each player on the winning team is allowed to keep the Cup for one day. So, despite its stature, the Cup has been on some strange adventures. It has spent time as a planter for geraniums, a dish for ice cream sundaes, and a feed bowl for a Kentucky Derby winner!

On the day of the Heritage Classic, 57,167 fans swept into the stands to watch history in action. Despite the severe cold, fans cheered with excitement as the Legends Game began. People were thrilled to see Gretzky and other hockey greats lacing up their skates. The game was lively, and players even picked up shovels to clear ice shavings between periods.

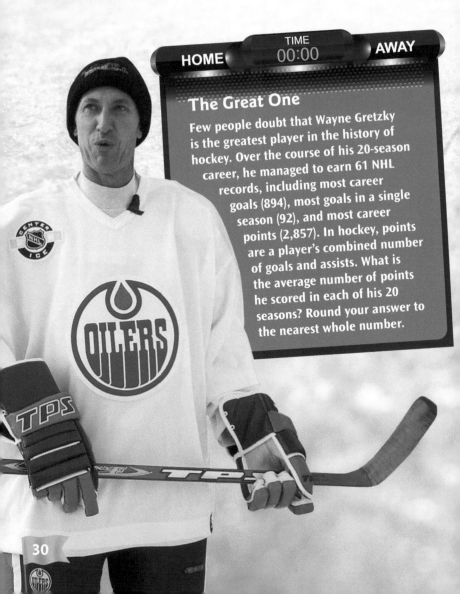

TIME
00:00
HOME
AWAY

The Great One

Few people doubt that Wayne Gretzky is the greatest player in the history of hockey. Over the course of his 20-season career, he managed to earn 61 NHL records, including most career goals (894), most goals in a single season (92), and most career points (2,857). In hockey, points are a player's combined number of goals and assists. What is the average number of points he scored in each of his 20 seasons? Round your answer to the nearest whole number.

Bundle Up!

Do you wish you had attended this once-in-a-lifetime game? You would have needed your warmest winter coat, two pairs of thermal underwear, and at least three pairs of thick socks. The temperature on game day was a bone-chilling −22°F (−30°C)!

The regular season game between the Oilers and the Canadiens ended with the Oilers losing 4–3. But even the loss could not drag down the fans' spirits, many of whom had braved the cold for more than six hours. They knew they had witnessed something special.

Outdoor NHL games are more frequent now because of the success of the 2003 Heritage Classic. However, one can argue that nothing will ever top that **inaugural** game. Gretzky called the experience "one of the great days of my life"—an opinion shared by most people involved.

History's Most Crowded Soccer Stadium

How many people do you suppose could fit in a soccer stadium? You have to look back to 1950 for the highest number. That year, Brazil hosted the Federation Internationale de Football Association (FIFA) World Cup final in Rio de Janeiro's Maracanã Stadium. People from all over the world came to Brazil to watch the match. The word crowded took on a whole new meaning that day!

Exactly how many people were crammed into the stands that day in Brazil? There were a whopping 173,850 people in the stadium! What's even more astonishing is that the number only accounts for fans with paid tickets. There were even more people who snuck into the stadium without tickets. Many people believe the actual number of spectators was closer to 220,000.

Ticket Trade

Brazilian Joedir Belmont was one of the lucky ticketholders to the famous match, but he never got to see the game. He stayed home to take care of his ill mother. Nearly 65 years later, Belmont donated his unused ticket to the FIFA museum. In thanks, FIFA gave him tickets to the 2014 World Cup finals, which also took place in Brazil.

Fútbol Fanatics

In 2011, the 51,998 *fútbol* (soccer in Spanish) fans at the Turk Telekon Arena in Istanbul, Turkey, cheered at a level that made it one of the loudest stadiums in the world. The crowd's roar got as loud as 131.76 decibels. That's nearly the same as a jet engine at takeoff!

Uruguayan goalkeeper diving for a Brazilian shot that went wide

Why Was It So Crowded?

Back in 1950, Brazil was given the opportunity to host the first FIFA World Cup in 12 years. The people of Brazil were honored to host the World Cup—not only because it was the first since before World War II, but also because the Brazilian soccer team was thought to be one of the top contenders. The Cup was sure to attract a massive number of spectators. To prepare for the crowds, the Maracanã Stadium was built especially for the World Cup.

The final match was a legendary contest between Brazil and Uruguay. The people of Brazil were ecstatic that their team had made it to the finals. A victory on home soil looked within reach. This combination led to an incredible record for the largest number of fans at a sporting event— and the most cramped stadium in the world!

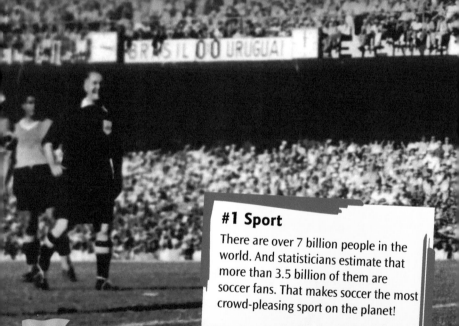

#1 Sport

There are over 7 billion people in the world. And statisticians estimate that more than 3.5 billion of them are soccer fans. That makes soccer the most crowd-pleasing sport on the planet!

And the Winner Is . . .

Despite the phenomenal cheering section, a victory for Brazil was not meant to be. Brazil lost to Uruguay 2–1.

The Three-Day Tennis Match

During Wimbledon on June 22, 2010, anticipation hung thick in the air. John Isner of the United States and France's Nicolas Mahut walked on to the court at 6:13 p.m. for a match they thought would conclude by sunset. Fans crowded into the stands, eager to watch two top tennis players compete.

No one had any idea they were settling in for history's longest tennis match.

John Isner and Nicolas Mahut

Game, Set, Match!

A tennis match is made up of games and sets. To win a game, a player must score at least three points and be two points ahead of an opponent. Then, a player needs to win a minimum of six games. For the match, a player needs to win two out of three games. The exception in some men's professional tournaments is that a player must win three out of five games.

Day 1

The match started off in a fairly routine manner. Isner won the first set 6–4 in 32 minutes, but Mahut quickly bounced back, winning the next two sets. Only 29 minutes were spent on the second set, while it took Mahut 49 minutes to win 7–6 in the third set.

The fourth set ran the longest on the first day, lasting 64 minutes before Isner won. The two opponents were tied with two sets each, and all eyes were on the deciding final set. However, the day was getting late and light was fading fast. The decision was made to suspend play until the next day, and a conclusion to the match seemed just beyond the horizon.

| HOME | TIME 00:00 | AWAY |

It's All about Speed

Samuel Groth of Australia is responsible for the fastest recorded tennis serve in the world. On May 9, 2012, his swift serve clocked in at 163.4 miles per hour! If the tennis ball magically traveled for 3 hours at that same speed, what would be the total distance the ball traveled?

Day 2

Neither player was willing to let the match slip out of reach. To win a set, you must win at least two games more than your opponent—and neither Isner nor Mahut would **concede** defeat!

The hours began to march by. At 5:45 p.m. on Day 2, the match was officially the longest in history, with the score of the fifth set standing at 32 games each! There seemed to be no end in sight.

By 9:10 p.m., officials were forced to suspend play again. At this point, the score of the set was an **astronomical** 59–59, and the two men had been playing against each other for more than seven hours over two days.

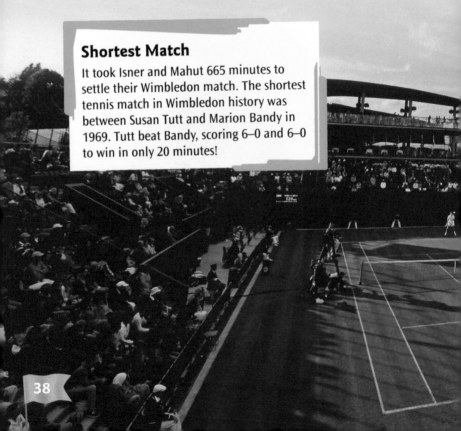

Shortest Match

It took Isner and Mahut 665 minutes to settle their Wimbledon match. The shortest tennis match in Wimbledon history was between Susan Tutt and Marion Bandy in 1969. Tutt beat Bandy, scoring 6–0 and 6–0 to win in only 20 minutes!

Day 3

Back and forth, Isner and Mahut continued the *thwack-thwack* of a captivating set. Finally, an hour and seven minutes into play on the third day, Isner served the match point and won the game. The final score was an astounding 70–68.

It took Isner and Mahut 11 hours and 5 minutes (and 183 games) to declare a victor in the match of a lifetime. It was a trial that tested their physical and mental strengths, one that has been memorialized in countless articles and record books. Rest assured, this is a tennis match that will not be forgotten.

Grand Slams

These four tournaments are the most **reputable** in the tennis world and offer the most prize money for players.

U.S. Open
National Tennis Center
Queens, New York

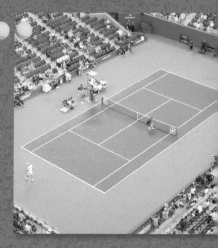

- based on the U.S. National Championship, which began in 1881
- played in late summer each year
- Arthur Ashe—1997, stadium named in his honor as the first African American winner of the men's singles

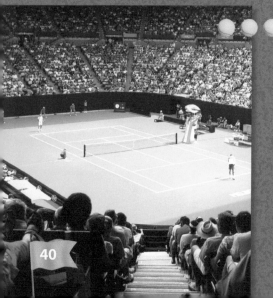

Australian Open
Melbourne Park
Melbourne, Australia

- began in 1905 and reached major status in 1924
- played in January each year
- Ken Rosewall—the youngest and oldest men's singles champion at ages 18 and 37

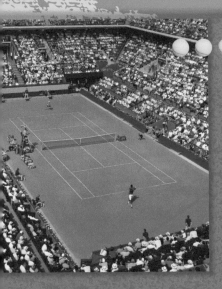

French Open
Roland Garros
Paris, France

- began in 1891
- played in spring each year
- Althea Gibson—the first African American woman to win the women's singles in 1956

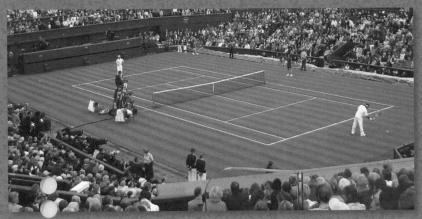

Wimbledon
All England Lawn Tennis & Croquet Club
London, England

- began in 1877
- played in early summer each year
- players must wear almost all white attire

A Celebration of Inspiration

Startling statistics, legendary winning streaks, **inconceivable** comebacks, and games that stretched over days. These are what unforgettable sports moments are made of—and new moments like these are happening all the time!

Most of these stories live on as legends, retold by avid fans and shared with new generations. The legends all begin in truth, and the truth stems from the best that sports has to offer— the drive of teamwork or individual grit. Most importantly, the stories endure from the pure joy of loving sports.

When young players step up to the plate, put on a helmet, or lace their cleats, they should keep these stories in mind. The stories will remind them that **perseverance** can get a person anywhere in the sporting world. Who knows— maybe one day an athlete just like you will become the stuff of legends—or the next chapter in a book.

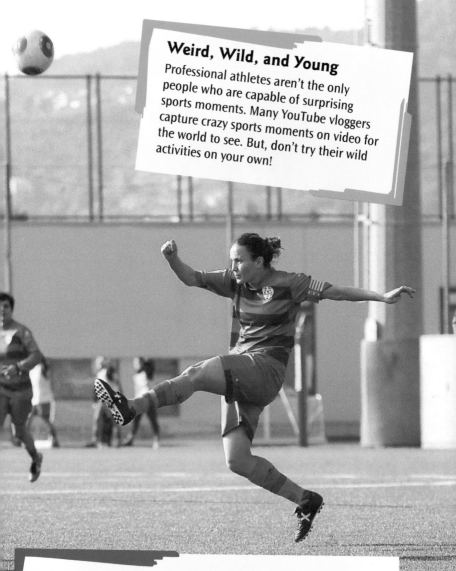

Weird, Wild, and Young

Professional athletes aren't the only people who are capable of surprising sports moments. Many YouTube vloggers capture crazy sports moments on video for the world to see. But, don't try their wild activities on your own!

Women's Leagues

Although sports such as football and baseball don't have professional leagues for women, there are a number of others that do, including the WNBA, Women's Tennis Association (WTA), National Women's Soccer League (NWSL), Ladies Professional Golf Association (LPGA), and National Women's Hockey League (NWHL).

Glossary

adrenaline—a hormone released when frightened, excited, or angered that speeds up heart rate and increases blood flow

anticipation—the excitement of looking forward to an event, someone, or something

astronomical—massive in quantity

brine—saturated salt water

concede—to surrender or give up

deficit—number of points a team is behind the opponent's score

feat—great accomplishment

inaugural—the launch of a new activity or event

inconceivable—mind-boggling, impossible

infamous—well-known for something bad

intercepted—when the opposing team caught the ball instead of the team with possession

momentum—the act of gaining speed, forward motion, and active force

on-base percentages—baseball statistics that are calculated based on how often the players reach first base

perseverance—continued effort in pursuit of a difficult accomplishment

pipe rig—plastic pipes joined together

pitted—competed against

possession—one team has complete control of the ball

pristine—perfectly clean

regulation—the regular period of time to play a game

reinvented—a renewed way of doing something

reputable—well-respected

statisticians—people who collect individual and/or team data in sports

symmetrical—perfectly regular and even in terms of shape

unpredictable—an event that you cannot guess the outcome of

wild card—football term referring to the non-division winners that qualify for playoffs

wonky—very weird

Index

Check It Out!

Books

Alexander, Kwame. 2014. *The Crossover*. HMH Books for Young Readers.

Birmingham, Maria. 2013. *WeirdZone: Sports*. Owlkids Books.

Bow, Patricia. 2009. *Tennis Science*. Crabtree Publishing Company.

Buckley, James, Jr. 2010. *The Ultimate Guide to Baseball*. Franklin Watts.

_____. 2010. *The Ultimate Guide to Football*. Franklin Watts.

Thomas, Keltie. 2005. *How Basketball Works*. Owlkids Books.

Van Draanen, Wendelin. 2012. *The Running Dream*. Ember.

Websites

Federation Internationale de Football Association. http://www.fifa.com.

Major League Baseball. http://www.mlb.com.

National Basketball Association. http://www.nba.com.

National Football League. http://www.nfl.com.

National Hockey League. http://www.nhl.com.

Wimbledon. *About the All England Club and the Championships*. http://www.wimbledon.com/en_GB/about_wimbledon/index.html.

Women's National Basketball Association. http://www.wnba.com.

Try It!

Imagine that you're a sportscaster and you have the chance to report on one of the record-breaking contests described in this book. Decide which of these incredible events to share and how you would report it.

- When and where did this event take place?

- What sport was being played?

- What teams were involved?

- What were some highlights from the game?

- What records were broken?

About the Author

Monika Davies is a Canadian writer and a huge fan of all winter sports, including hockey, curling, and ice skating. Being Canadian, she is not afraid of blizzards, knows how to build a perfect snowman, and owns five pairs of winter boots. Unfortunately, she does not know how to skate, though her sister promises to teach her. (That probably won't happen.) Monika graduated from the University of British Columbia with a Bachelor of Fine Arts in creative writing.

Answers

page 5—45%

page 7—approximately 250 days

page 11—5.8%; 33.1% (commercial time); 35.1% (shots of players)

page 17—2,873

page 21—78 minutes

page 25—1. As the player's height increases, so does his shoe size. 2. Magic Johnson and Yao Ming have shoe sizes that would be considered outliers. They are outliers because their plot points on the graph do not match with the upward trajectory of the other plot points. 3. Individual players: 7.41 (Bogues), 6.57 (Robinson), 5.75 (Thomas), 6 (Jordan), 5.57 (Bryant). Answer is 6.26, which is an approximate ratio of shoe size to height for basketball players.

page 30—143 points per season

page 37—491 miles

CPSIA information can be obtained
at www.ICGtesting.com
Printed in the USA
LVHW070844071121
702656LV00001B/18